INSTRUMENTS OF SCIENCE

George Homatidis

Literacy Consultants
David Booth • Kathleen Corrigan

Contents

NECESSARY INVENTIONS

Humans have used tools for millions of years. At first, tools were used for survival. In the Stone Age, stone axes and spears were used for hunting food. Later, as people began living in organized societies, tools were developed for building larger **structures**. For example, the pulley was invented for lifting heavy weights using wheels and ropes.

As people evolved, they sought to understand and explain the natural world. They did this by looking for patterns in things and events and by asking questions: How do plants grow? How are clouds formed? What is the sun? How do planets move?

Illustration of a steam hammer being used in a foundry

Understanding these things required the development of more sophisticated tools. Tools like rulers and balance scales were created for measuring length and weight. Lenses and telescopes were invented for viewing and observing objects near and far. Much later, cameras and computers were invented for displaying and recording the details of observations that were made.

Over the centuries, scientists, inventors, and engineers built on one another's work to develop and refine the necessary tools for further scientific breakthroughs. It was truly a case of "necessity is the mother of invention."

HOW WE

MEASURE

There are many devices for measuring the relationship between two objects, such as distance, and many devices for measuring the physical properties of objects, such as weight and temperature. **Accurate** measurements allow us to compare different objects using concrete numbers and descriptions.

Distance

You've probably used a ruler in class to measure short distances, for instance, the distance between your desk and the classroom door. However, to measure minute, or very small, distances, you use a micrometer. A micrometer is a mechanical instrument that measures the distance or the thickness between its two plates. A micrometer can measure the diameter of a very small hole or the thickness of a sheet of paper.

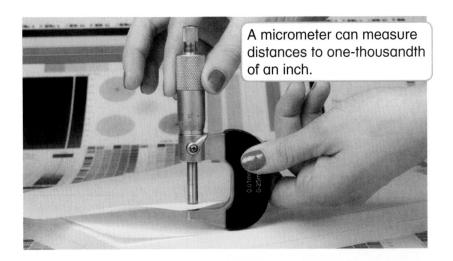

A micrometer can measure distances to one-thousandth of an inch.

A laser's concentrated beam can cut precise designs into metal, wood, plastic, fabric, and many other materials.

On the other hand, to measure very long distances, for instance, the distance to the moon, scientists need a laser. A laser is a highly **concentrated** high-energy beam. To measure something from far away, a laser is pointed at the distant object. The beam travels at the speed of light to the object, bounces off the object, and returns. Since the speed of light is known, by measuring the time it takes for the beam to return, scientists can calculate the distance to the faraway object.

A laser has many other applications. It can be used as a cutting tool, used for recording and playing CDs and DVDs, and even used for repairing a person's retina during eye surgery.

Safety Note

You may be familiar with small, handheld lasers used as pointers; perhaps you've seen them in your classroom. Whatever the size of the laser, remember to use it with care and never point it at a person. A laser's concentrated beam can cause damage to the eyes.

Weight

Weight is the measurement of gravity's pull on an object. The most commonly used units of measurement for weight on Earth are the pound and kilogram.

To find out the weight of an object on Earth, we can use a simple scale. Typical bathroom and grocery store scales are spring scales. They work by measuring how much a spring **compresses** or stretches when an object's weight is acted upon it. These scales are useful for measuring everyday things, but they are not the most accurate.

The springs in a bathroom scale compress when measuring weight.

Did You Know?

Since we live on Earth, our weight is directly related to Earth's gravity. Therefore, if you were to stand on another planet, your weight would change according to the gravity of that planet. For example, if you weighed 90 pounds on Earth, you would weigh about 34 pounds on Mars and about 212 pounds on Jupiter!

Sometimes scientists need to measure precise amounts of an ingredient. For these purposes, laboratories use analytical scales that can cost tens of thousands of dollars. These scales are precise enough to measure the weight of a single grain of sugar. Analytical scales are especially important tools in medicine. When measuring chemicals used in medicine, the slightest inaccuracy could mean the difference between life and death.

Analytical scales can measure objects weighing less than one milligram. The weighing platform is sometimes protected from air turbulence by a glass shield.

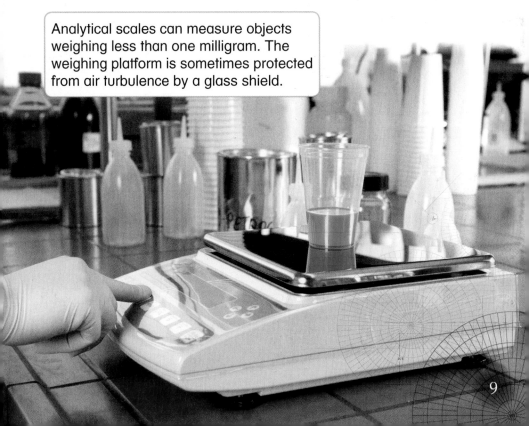

WHEELS AND PULLEYS

Acrobats and actors use pulley systems to create flying effects onstage.

One of the first great inventions was the wheel. The wheel allowed humans to **construct** vehicles for carrying heavy objects or people over long distances.

The wheel also gave rise to other tools, such as the pulley. A pulley can be used for moving loads that are extremely heavy or hard to reach. A single pulley consists of a wheel with a groove around which you loop a rope or a cable. The load is attached to one end of the rope. As you pull down — apply force — on the other end of the rope, the wheel moves and lifts the load up. If you have more than one pulley working together — a system of pulleys — less force is needed to move the load.

Fixed pulley

System of two pulleys

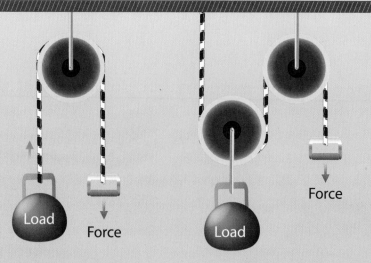

Load

Force

Load

Force

Mercury-in-glass thermometers were created in the 1700s.

Temperature

A thermometer is an instrument for measuring temperature. It can be used to tell the temperature of gases, liquids, and even solids, for instance whether your body temperature is too high when you're sick.

A traditional thermometer is a glass tube with markings on the side. Inside it contains a very thin tube with a bulb at the bottom. The bulb is filled with either a liquid metal — mercury — or alcohol with a red dye to make it easy to see. As the temperature increases, the liquid expands and rises inside the inner tube. Where it stops is the temperature of whatever is being measured.

There are two scales in use for everyday thermometers: the Celsius scale, which is used in most countries, and the Fahrenheit scale, which is used in the United States.

Did You Know?

Electronic thermometers use a microchip instead of mercury to measure body temperature.

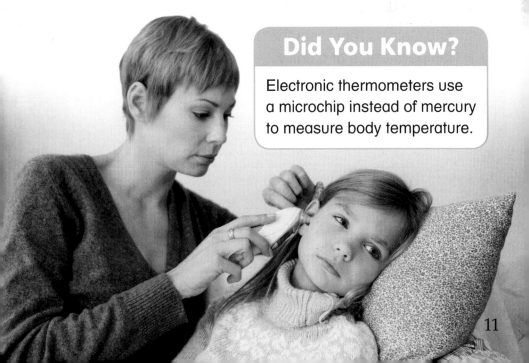

FAHRENHEIT VS. CELSIUS

Daniel Gabriel Fahrenheit was a German physicist working in the 1700s. He developed the Fahrenheit scale using a mixture of ice and salt, with the freezing point of that mixture being 0°F. The freezing point of pure water was eventually measured at 32°F, and its boiling point was measured at 212°F. The difference between these two points is 180 degrees.

Also working in the 1700s, Swedish astronomer Anders Celsius used the freezing point of pure water as 0°C and the boiling point as 100°C. This difference of 100 was divided into equal parts to produce the Celsius scale.

The difference between Fahrenheit and Celsius can be startling. In Fahenheit, 30 degrees is below freezing, but in Celsius, 30 degrees is actually very warm. The only time Fahrenheit and Celsius represent the same temperature is at a chilly minus 40 degrees.

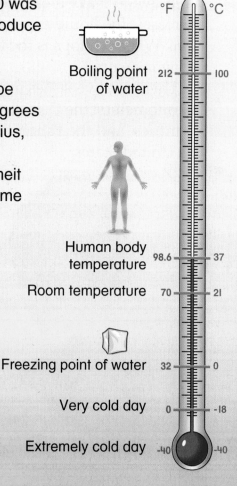

°F °C

Boiling point of water 212 — 100

Human body temperature 98.6 — 37

Room temperature 70 — 21

Freezing point of water 32 — 0

Very cold day 0 — -18

Extremely cold day -40 — -40

Speedometer

Speed, Height, and More

Other measuring tools help us to learn more about how an object performs or to find out more about the world around us. You might be familiar with the speedometer in a car. This tells you how fast a vehicle is going and helps to keep roads safe. An altimeter is used in airplanes to measure how high an airplane is flying. A photometer is built into every camera, including the camera in a phone, to measure and control the amount of light hitting the camera sensor.

These are only a few of the many measuring tools available for everyday use as well as for scientific experiments. In addition, measuring tools are often combined with other tools or instruments to help us observe, study, and record the world around us.

Altimeter in an airplane

13

HOW WE
OBSERVE

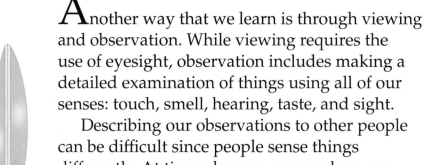

Another way that we learn is through viewing and observation. While viewing requires the use of eyesight, observation includes making a detailed examination of things using all of our senses: touch, smell, hearing, taste, and sight.

Describing our observations to other people can be difficult since people sense things differently. At times, human senses alone are simply not **adequate**. To improve our abilities at observation, tools and instruments have been developed to sharpen our senses or to help us sense things that we normally cannot.

Convex
lens

Concave
lens

Lenses

Lenses are used in a great number of instruments to help us see things not easily visible to the human eye.

A lens is a **transparent** piece of plastic, glass, or other material with at least one curved surface. There are two main types of lenses. A convex lens looks a lot like a lentil in shape. The glass or plastic surfaces are thicker in the middle than at the top and bottom. A concave lens is exactly the opposite. The concave lens is thinner in the middle and thicker at the top and bottom.

A lens works by refraction. What this means is that the lens bends the light rays in a different direction as the light rays pass through it.

A convex lens makes light rays bend and converge, or come together, at a point behind the lens. This point is called the focal point, or more simply, the focus. Human eyes are naturally convex lenses. Magnifying glasses are also examples of convex lenses.

Parallel Rays of Light

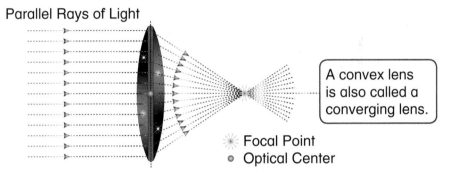

A convex lens is also called a converging lens.

☀ Focal Point
◉ Optical Center

A concave lens makes the incoming light rays diverge, or spread out. If you look through a concave lens, the focal point seems to appear in front of the lens at a point where the light rays meet. Concave lenses are used in things such as flashlights, car headlights, and cinema projectors.

Parallel Rays of Light

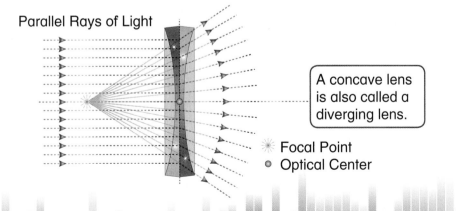

A concave lens is also called a diverging lens.

☀ Focal Point
◉ Optical Center

SEEING THINGS

Some people's eyes cannot focus light on the retina properly, which leads to blurred vision. Eyeglasses can correct that. People who are farsighted can see distant things more clearly than near ones. They need eyeglasses with convex lenses, which bend light more sharply and help them focus on close-up objects. People who are nearsighted are able to see near things more clearly than distant ones. They need glasses made with concave lenses, which bend light outward and help them see distant objects more clearly.

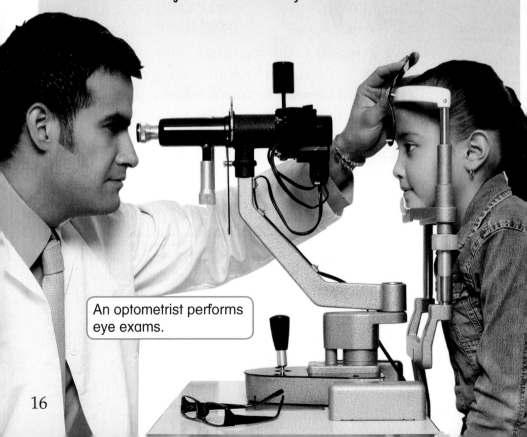

An optometrist performs eye exams.

A SIMPLE EXPERIMENT

To make a simple lens, you will need:

- an old newspaper or magazine
- a piece of clear plastic
- an eyedropper
- water

Follow the five simple steps described below:

1 Take an old newspaper or magazine.

2 Lay a small piece of clear plastic over the paper.

3 Use an eyedropper to place a small drop of water on the plastic.

4 Look at the print under the water drop. What do you see?

5 Lift the plastic away from the paper or make the drop larger. What do you see now?

Tools With Lenses

In order to better observe our world, sometimes we can use more than one lens at the same time or combine the two types of lenses together in an instrument.

A simple convex lens makes small things look bigger. A magnifying glass is an example of a simple convex lens. To study even smaller things, a microscope is used. A microscope helps us observe and learn about tiny objects, such as human cells, or parts of an object, such as the little veins of a leaf. A typical compound microscope you might use in school has convex lenses for stronger magnification.

Lenses are also what make binoculars work. Binoculars help us see things that are far away. They are useful for many things, for example, observing and learning about birds in flight and letting us study the behaviors of animals from a safe distance.

Microscopic view of a leaf

There are different binoculars for different viewing activities. Make sure to get the right one for your needs.

For viewing distant objects such as the planets, a telescope is used. A Dutch eyeglass maker named Hans Lippershey is credited with creating the first telescope in 1608. The telescope combines a number of lenses to enhance the size, brightness, and clarity of faraway things. It is a simple tool that helped to change our view of Earth and the universe forever.

Today we have very powerful telescopes. Some of these are put on the top of mountains and use enormous lenses and mirrors to let us see very far away. In 1990 the Hubble Space Telescope was put into orbit high above Earth. It has given us some of the most remarkable images of the universe.

The Hubble Space Telescope captured an image of a mountain of dust and gas, "Mystic Mountain," in the Carina Nebula, 7,500 light-years from Earth.

The Hubble Space Telescope remains in operation to this day.

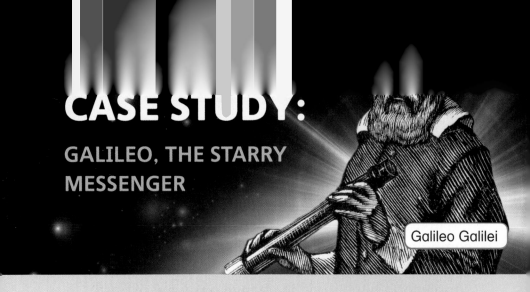

CASE STUDY:

GALILEO, THE STARRY MESSENGER

Galileo Galilei

Galileo Galilei (1564–1642) was a very influential Italian astronomer, physicist, and philosopher. He made many **contributions** to science, among them the telescope.

In 1609 Galileo heard about Hans Lippershey's invention of the telescope. Without having seen the original, Galileo constructed a better version, which was nearly three times more powerful. Although his version of the telescope was not as powerful as today's telescopes, it allowed Galileo to study the motion of the planets.

Galileo was the first to use a telescope for astronomical observation. He discovered that the moon had mountains and valleys; it was not smooth, as everyone had first thought. He named four of the moons of Jupiter and observed **phenomena** such as sunspots and the phases of the planet Venus.

The sun is the center of the solar system.

Using his telescope, Galileo proved that the sun, not Earth, was at the center of the solar system. He did so by observing the planets' patterns of movement. Galileo built upon the work of Nicolaus Copernicus and Johannes Kepler, two earlier astronomers and mathematicians who had proposed the theory that the sun was at the center of the solar system. Copernicus and Kepler had not published their theories when they were alive because they were afraid that they would be put on trial. At that time, the opinion was that Earth was the center of the solar system.

Galileo's work put him in direct opposition to the opinions of most people and to the views of the Catholic Church. He was condemned for **heresy**, a very serious crime at the time. Galileo was sentenced to permanent house arrest.

It took another 500 years before the Church cleared Galileo of this charge.

The moon's surface is covered with mountains and valleys.

The word "stethoscope" comes from the Greek words *stethos*, meaning "chest," and *skopein*, meaning "to explore."

Other Observation Tools

Observation tools help us understand what things are made of and how they work. Doctors use a stethoscope to listen to sounds inside the body. A stethoscope can tell your doctor if your lungs and heart are working properly. A periscope is used by people in submarines to look above the surface of the water. A fluoroscope uses X rays to take "movies" of the inner structures of **opaque** objects in motion. A spectroscope works a lot like a prism. It breaks up visible light into its different **component** colors. This is very important because we can tell what an object is made of by looking at the different colors coming from it.

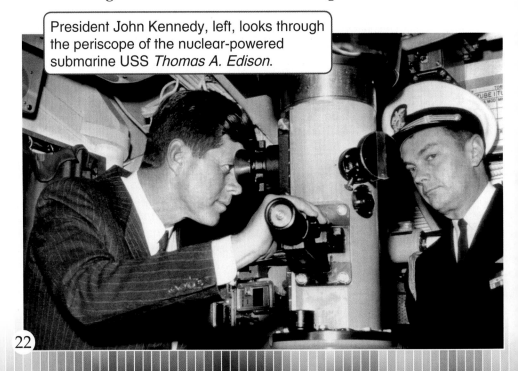

President John Kennedy, left, looks through the periscope of the nuclear-powered submarine USS *Thomas A. Edison*.

ZHANG HENG'S SEISMOSCOPE

Around the year 132 C.E., a Chinese scientist named Zhang Heng invented the world's first known seismoscope to detect earthquakes from far away. Zhang's seismoscope was a bronze jar with eight bronze dragons arranged around the outside. Each dragon faced one of the eight principal directions of a compass and held a loose metal ball in its mouth. Below each dragon was a bronze toad with its mouth agape. When an earthquake occurred, the dragon facing the direction of the earthquake would drop its ball. The toad below would catch the ball, making a loud clinking noise.

Scientists believe the inside of Zhang's seismoscope contained a pendulum. An earthquake would cause the pendulum to swing in that particular direction, triggering a dragon to drop its ball. This instrument was reportedly able to detect earthquakes from 400 miles away. Early detection allowed the government to quickly send help to the disaster zone.

Pendulum

A model of Zhang's seismoscope

HOW WE
DOCUMENT

In addition to measuring the properties of things and accurately observing natural events, we need to be able to display and record our findings. This is so that we can share information with other people in a concrete way.

Camera

A camera lens is made up of a number of individual lenses. A camera uses these lenses to focus the light that bounces back from an object. By doing this, it gives us an image of that object. Apart from taking everyday pictures, a camera can be used as a scientific tool. A camera can, for example, be attached to a microscope or a telescope. This allows us to share images of very small or faraway objects with people who do not have a microscope or telescope available.

The image produced by a microscope is picked up by the sensor of the camera.

1960s

1970s

Computer

A computer can be used for activities such as playing video games or watching movies. The computer is also a very powerful scientific tool. It can take images from various sources and display them on a screen. It allows us to send and receive files to and from other people working on similar projects. A computer also allows us to go on the Internet to research any subject. This kind of fast and easy access was unthinkable just a few decades ago.

1980s

1990s

Caution!

Don't believe everything you read online. Make sure that the information comes from a respected Web site. You should always double-check any information with at least one other source.

2000s

2010s

2016

Modern polygraph machines use computers to record the data.

Recording Tools

Professionals from many fields rely on recording tools. For example, law enforcement officials use a polygraph, which is a lie detector, to measure and record small changes in the pulse and breathing of a person taking a polygraph test. Although it's not a perfectly accurate instrument, a polygraph can often help an experienced technician tell whether someone is lying.

Recording tools are used widely in medicine. You might have heard of an electrocardiograph, which is used to record the natural electrical activity of the heart. An electroencephalograph records the natural electrical activity of the brain. In both cases, the recording machines change the electrical signals received into patterns that can be seen on a screen as a series of lines.

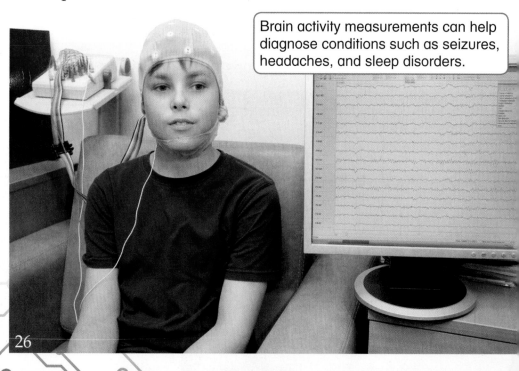

Brain activity measurements can help diagnose conditions such as seizures, headaches, and sleep disorders.

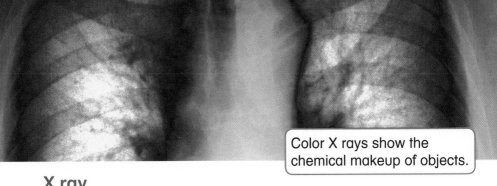

X ray

One of the great medical breakthroughs of the late 1800s and early 1900s was the invention of radiography. Radiography is a technique that uses radiation to see and record the internal structures of an object. A radiograph is better known as an image made by an X-ray machine.

In 1895 Wilhelm Röntgen discovered some mysterious rays that could not only pass through skin and muscles but could also make images of human bones. He called these X rays. An "X" is used to represent something that's unknown.

X rays are in wide use today in the field of medicine. They make it possible for us to see inside the body as well as to treat tumors. X rays are also used by geologists to study rocks and by botanists to look at the inner structures of plants.

Many scientists contributed to the development of radiography. A lot of the credit, however, belongs to one of the greatest modern scientists: Marie Curie.

Dental X rays show the health of the teeth and bones, and of the soft tissues around them.

CASE STUDY:
MARIE CURIE

Marie Curie

Marie Sklodowska (1867–1934) is better known by her married name, Marie Curie. She was born in Warsaw, Poland, and was an exceptional student from an early age. At that time, women in Poland weren't allowed to go to university. In order to continue her education, she went to Paris, where she met and married Pierre Curie, also a scientist.

In 1893 Marie Curie earned a master's degree in physics. A year later, she also completed a master's degree in math. Continuing her education, she decided to study the rays produced by the element uranium. She was inspired by French scientist Henri Becquerel's discovery that rays from uranium could pass through metal. Her research involved the examination of many substances and minerals for similar activity. She found that a uranium ore called pitchblende gave off more radioactive rays than pure uranium. She concluded that pitchblende must contain other chemical elements that were more radioactive than uranium. And she was right.

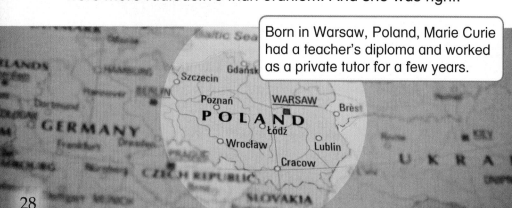

Born in Warsaw, Poland, Marie Curie had a teacher's diploma and worked as a private tutor for a few years.

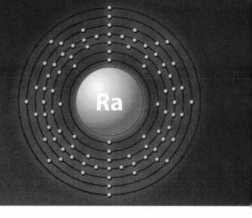

Radium is used in the treatment of cancer and in therapies for other diseases.

This mystery element was radium, a substance a million times more radioactive than uranium. Radium was one of two elements discovered by Marie Curie and her husband. The other was polonium, named by Marie Curie to honor her homeland. Marie Curie coined the term "radioactivity" to describe this emission of active rays. In 1903 she presented a doctoral thesis on radioactive substances, for which she was awarded the Nobel Prize in Physics. She shared the prize with her husband, Pierre, and Henri Becquerel.

In 1910, after years of painstaking work, Marie Curie produced a pure sample of the element radium. For this, she was awarded the 1911 Nobel Prize in Chemistry. She is the only person ever to have won Nobel Prizes in Physics and in Chemistry.

Marie and Pierre Curie worked together in a laboratory in Paris, France.

Did You Know?

Marie Curie died in July 1934 from a blood disease. It's likely that the radioactivity she was exposed to during her career caused the disease.

HOW WE
IMPROVE

Many of the tools described work together to give us a complete picture of what things are made of and how they work. These tools also provide readings and images for us to share.

From the simple wheel to advanced telescopes, the evolution of scientific instruments has gone hand in hand with the development of humans. Tools were developed to help humans measure, observe, and document our world. As we continue to advance and interact with our environment, the future of scientific tools will undoubtedly bring many more fascinating developments.

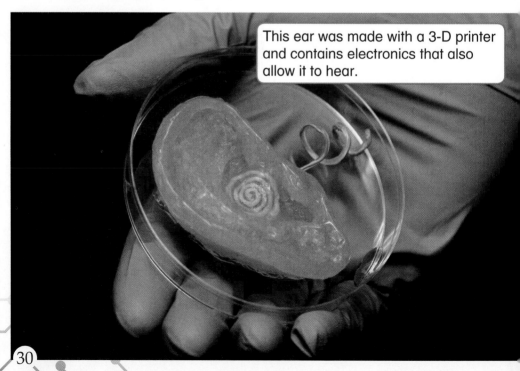

This ear was made with a 3-D printer and contains electronics that also allow it to hear.

MEASURE

Increasing amounts of indoor and outdoor air pollution around the world are causing significant health problems, such as asthma, in people. Commercial air quality monitors measure levels of harmful substances in the air to help people understand, manage, and take action against air pollution.

OBSERVE

Farmers are increasingly using drones to survey crop growth and crop health. Airborne cameras on agricultural drones can take infrared pictures of crops and help expose infestation problems that can't be seen with the naked eye.

DOCUMENT

Compact and convenient, the modern smartphone has a wide range of practical applications. A growing number of smartphone applications let users track and record heart rate, sleep patterns, and even the number of steps taken in a day. Documentation of such information can help users improve their health and fitness habits.

Glossary

accurate: free from errors; exact

adequate: satisfactory; acceptable

component: a part of something

compresses: squeezes together to take up less space

concentrated: intense

construct: build or make something

contributions: actions that help to bring about a result

heresy: a belief in something that goes against the accepted beliefs of a religion

opaque: not allowing light to pass through

phenomena: unusual or extraordinary circumstances, facts, or events

structures: anything composed of parts arranged in some way

transparent: allowing light to pass through

Index